D0229061

ART ATTACK

SECRET™ STUFF

with Neil Buchanan

A DORLING KINDERSLEY BOOK

DK

DORLING KINDERSLEY
LONDON, NEW YORK, MUNICH, PARIS,
MELBOURNE, DELHI

NORFOLK
LIBRARIES & INFORMATION SERVICE

480605	
PETERS	18-Mar-05
745.5	£9.99

Editor Penelope York
Designer Jacqueline Gooden

Prop Maker Jim Copley
Photography Steve Gorton, Gary Ombler

Managing Editor Mary Ling
Managing Art Editor Rachael Foster
Production Orla Creegan
DTP Designer Almudena Díaz
Jacket Designer Dean Price

Published in Great Britain by
Dorling Kindersley Limited
A Penguin Company
80 Strand, London, WC2R 0RL
4 6 8 10 9 7 5 3

Copyright © 2000 Dorling Kindersley Limited, London

All rights reserved. No part of this publication may be reproduced, stored in
a retrieval system, or transmitted in any form or by any means, electronic,
mechanical, photocopying, recording, or otherwise, without the prior
written permission of the copyright owner.

A CIP catalogue record for this book
is available from the British Library.

ISBN: 0-7513-7099-1

Colour reproduction by GRB Editrice S.r.l., Verona, Italy
Printed and bound in Italy by L.E.G.O.

Dorling Kindersley would like to thank everyone at
Media Merchants for their help and enthusiasm.
www.artattack.co.uk

For our complete catalogue visit
www.dk.com

CONTENTS

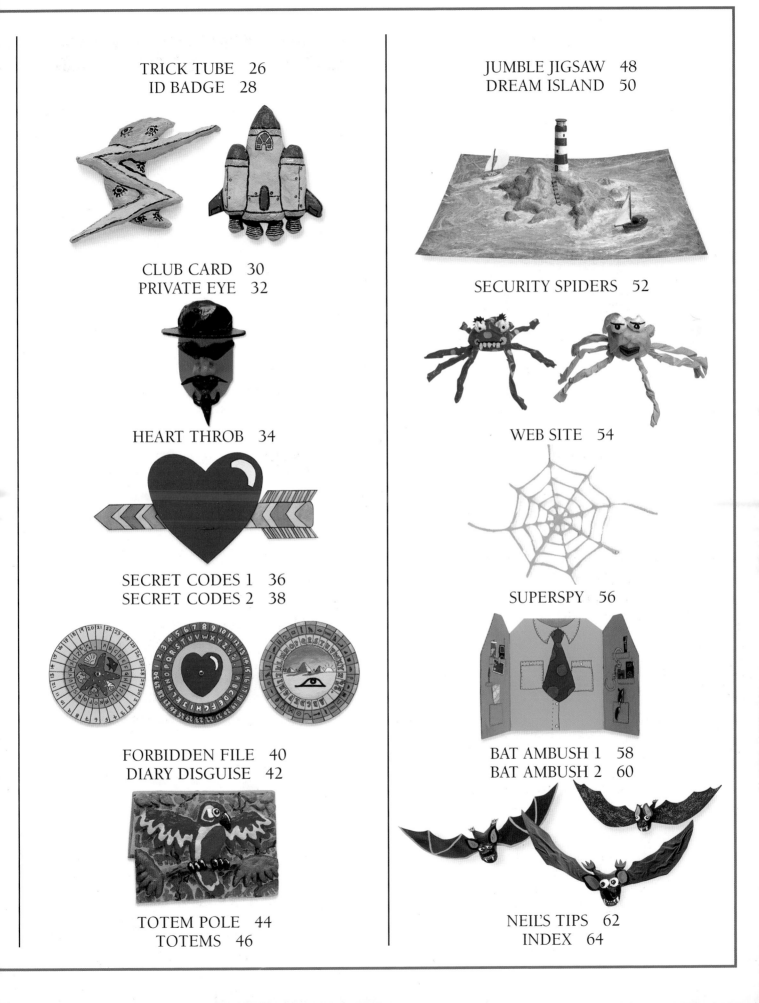

INTRODUCTION

Hello there! I see that you have broken into my new book of top secret Art Attacks! Use this book and I can assure you that no-one will find your hidden valuables and your room will be completely snooper-proof. The Art Attacks are all so easy to make that anyone can do them, so pulp up some PVA mixture, grab your paints, and have a top secret Art Attack! (But whatever you do, don't let anyone else in on the secret!)

NEIL BUCHANAN

Coloured card

Cardboard

Clingwrap

Cereal card

Paintbrushes

Coloured pencils

Coloured pens

Glitter

Party cups

Paints

Ribbon

Newspaper

Plastic bottle

Wrapping paper

Small boxes

Sticky tape

Bin-liners

Glue stick

Hints and tips
Look out for the exclamation marks. They appear throughout, giving you advice, hints, and tips for your 'secret stuff' projects.

Warning
★ Make sure you remember to open nearby windows before using marker pens.

★ Always be very careful when handling glue, and sharp objects such as scissors.

★ Remember to get permission before you start any of the projects in Art Attack Secret Stuff.

Ping-Pong balls

Scissors★

Art Attack bin
Make sure you save all the bits and pieces that your family leave lying around. Old boxes and toilet rolls may be just what you need for your Art Attacks!

Gold and silver pens★

Marker pens★

Wax Crayons

Glue Mixture
You will need to make this special glue mixture for many of the projects in the book. Twice as much PVA glue as water will make a strong mixture.

Two parts PVA glue

One part water

Finished glue mixture

5

GUARD DUTY

Have you ever been into your room and thought someone has been snooping? You know what you need . . . your own personal security guards!

From card to guard

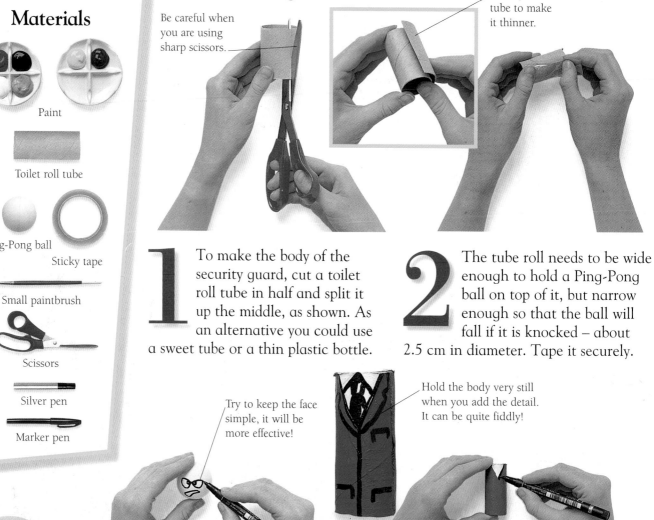

Be careful when you are using sharp scissors.

Roll up the tube to make it thinner.

Materials

Paint

Toilet roll tube

Ping-Pong ball

Sticky tape

Small paintbrush

Scissors

Silver pen

Marker pen

1 To make the body of the security guard, cut a toilet roll tube in half and split it up the middle, as shown. As an alternative you could use a sweet tube or a thin plastic bottle.

2 The tube roll needs to be wide enough to hold a Ping-Pong ball on top of it, but narrow enough so that the ball will fall if it is knocked – about 2.5 cm in diameter. Tape it securely.

Try to keep the face simple, it will be more effective!

Hold the body very still when you add the detail. It can be quite fiddly!

If you want colour on your Ping-Pong face, use acrylic paints.

3 Take a marker pen and draw a cartoon face on a Ping-Pong ball. Make it look slightly angry and comic looking! Paint the face with simple colours.

4 To make a uniform for your guards, paint the tube blue with a white 'v' shape at the front using acrylic paint. When the paint is dry, draw in the details with a black marker pen.

Secret code

In order to make the security guards do their job properly, you will need to make three of them and code them, as shown. Each day choose which head to put on which body and write down the combination, such as A-2, B-3, C-1. You can check later to see if they have been disturbed.

Security . . .

On the underside of each Ping-Pong head, draw the letter A, B, or C with a black marker pen. These will be hidden when the heads are on the bodies.

. . . conscious

Carefully draw a number, from one to three, on each of the arms of your security guards. Use a silver pen and outline it with a black marker pen.

Remember to write down the combination you have chosen when you put the guards into position. The codes will be useless if you forget them!

Try to make each guard have its own unique character by giving them different faces.

Make sure you draw in a tie and a shirt as the uniform, so your guards are well turned out.

Use silver pen to add details such as buttons and badges.

Practise drawing the faces on paper before you paint on to the heads.

GUARD DUTY

Now you have your own set of security guards complete with their own ingenious secret codes, guaranteed to completely snoop-proof your room! Try out your own designs, how about an Ant Attack!

These cheery ant expressions disguise the fact that they have a serious job to do!

Try sticking these antennae, made out of pipe-cleaners, on to your ants!

Why not make your favourite pop group or film stars into your guards!

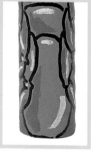

Remember to draw designs all the way around the bodies of your guards.

Security trap

Here's the clever bit! Just before you shut your door, pop your arm around it and place the bodies of your guards in a row. Then put the heads on top of the bodies making a note of which head is on which body. Now the trap is set! When you return to your room simply check to see if the codes have been disturbed. Make sure you don't knock them over yourself!

When the door opens the guards will fall down, and even if someone replaces them they won't know which head to put on to which body.

Add finer details to the bodies, such as the stripes on the legs to make the uniforms more realistic, and little hands the same colour as the heads.

Changing of the guards

Soldiers are just as good at guarding as security guards. Try making a whole regiment of army guards! The bright red uniforms and fierce faces will certainly make sure that anyone entering your room is caught red-handed!

To make the bearskin hats, dip some cotton wool in PVA glue, let it dry, then paint it black.

! **Trap tip**
Remember – when you leave the guards in position, write the code down somewhere so that you don't forget it when you return!

Shady characters

These tough looking individuals are the perfect snooper catchers. Their shifty dark glasses and aggressive expressions mean business! While they are not hard at work, why not put them on display in your room.

BOX OF TRICKS

Do you ever have trouble knowing what to send someone special? Here's an idea, a matchbox brooch, and what's inside? . . . shhh, it's a secret!

From box to brooch

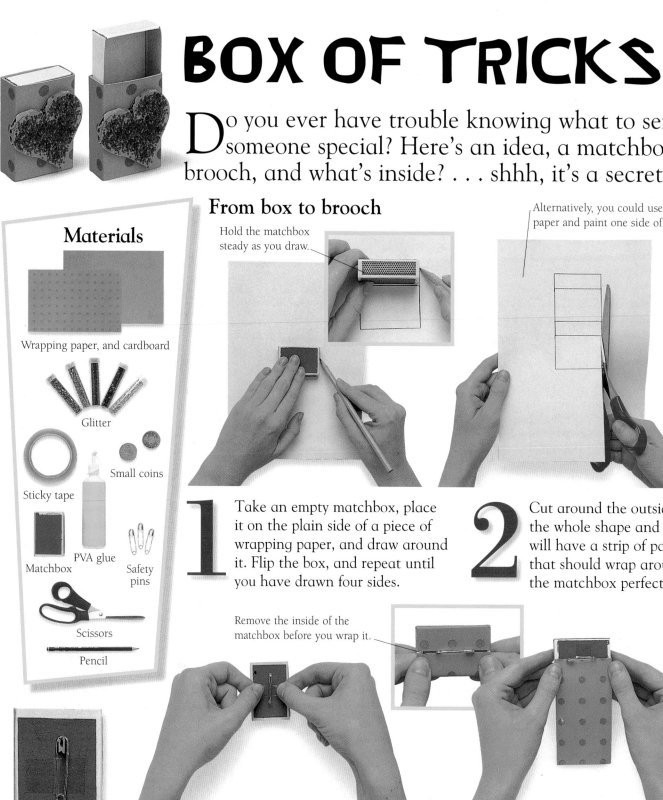

Materials

Wrapping paper, and cardboard

Glitter

Sticky tape

Small coins

PVA glue

Matchbox

Safety pins

Scissors

Pencil

Hold the matchbox steady as you draw.

Alternatively, you could use plain paper and paint one side of it.

1 Take an empty matchbox, place it on the plain side of a piece of wrapping paper, and draw around it. Flip the box, and repeat until you have drawn four sides.

2 Cut around the outside of the whole shape and you will have a strip of paper that should wrap around the matchbox perfectly.

Remove the inside of the matchbox before you wrap it.

Make sure the fastening of the safety pin is at the top.

3 Take a safety pin and slip some tape through the middle of it. Attach it to the matchbox so that it runs lengthways from the top to the bottom.

4 Cover the back of the piece of wrapping paper with PVA glue. Line up one end of the paper against the safety pin and wrap it around the matchbox until it arrives at the other side of the pin.

Mark a point that lines up with the middle of the coins. This will make the 'v' shape easier to draw.

If there are any gaps in the glitter, simply brush on a little more PVA glue and dip again!

Stick the heart on to the side that doesn't have the safety pin.

5 To draw the heart, take a stiff piece of card and place two small coins next to each other on it. Draw around the coins, and then a 'v' shape underneath them. Cut the heart shape out.

6 Brush both sides of the heart with PVA glue and dip it into some glitter. When it is dry, put a blob of PVA glue on to the front of the matchbox and stick the heart on firmly.

Close to the heart!

Now it's time to fill your matchbox! You could put a photo of yourself inside it for the person to wear near to their heart! Or you could write a secret letter or poem to pop inside.

Up, up, and away!

Why not make one for yourself? Design a special box and put a picture of your secret pin-up inside!

Football crazy

Try painting a football box for a special footie-fan friend. You could fill it with pictures of their favourite team players.

11

TREASURE TROVE

How about giving someone a present in a pirate treasure chest? Then hide the booty and give them a map (made on the next page) to find it!

From card to chest

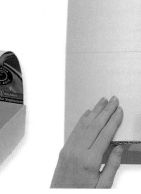

Attach the curved card to the sides of your shoe box lid.

Attach the cardboard ends with sticky tape.

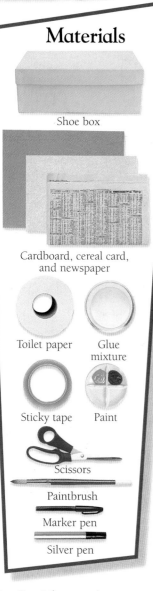

Materials

Shoe box

Cardboard, cereal card, and newspaper

Toilet paper

Glue mixture

Sticky tape

Paint

Scissors

Paintbrush

Marker pen

Silver pen

1 To make the lid of your chest, take a piece of cereal card and curve it over a shoe box lid as shown. Cut it down to size if necessary, and attach it with lots of sticky tape.

2 Place the lid on its end on a piece of cardboard and draw around the edge. Cut the arch shape out. Do the same for the other end. Stick the shapes to the sides.

! **Inside out**
Although it isn't necessary, it is a good idea to cover the inside of the box with newspaper as well. It will make the box stiffer and more secure.

3 Mix together some PVA glue mixture and paste it on to the lid and the box. Lay strips of newspaper all over both parts. You may want to do two or three layers. Make sure you cover the whole box.

4 When it is dry, add some detail using a marker pen. Mark the bolts that you would get on an old box and the metal strips that go along the lid. You will use these as guides to make the 3-D pulp decorations.

5 Dip scrunched up pieces of toilet paper into the PVA glue mixture and squeeze them out. Place them on the areas you marked previously. Make sure you put the pulp on the lid and box separately to ensure that they don't stick together – remember however, to make sure the lid still fits! Leave it to dry overnight.

6 Paint the treasure chest using poster or acrylic paint. Start by painting the whole thing with one base colour, and then paint on detail afterwards. Gold paint is very effective for the metal bolts and the keyhole, however, yellow would do just as well.

Stowaway present

Now that you have your treasure trove to hide your present inside, all you need is a map with an 'x marks the spot' showing where you have hidden it. Turn the page to find out how to make an authentic, ancient-looking treasure map and turn present-giving into hide and seek fun!

Wrap up your presents before you put them into the box.

When the box is dry, use silver pen to decorate the metal strips.

Add details, such as the wood effect, with a black marker pen.

Hide and seek

Simply wrap up the presents, pop them inside the chest and hide it carefully for the recipient to hunt down. Imagine how much more exciting it is to first receive a mysterious map then find your presents concealed in an authentic treasure chest!

TREASURE QUEST

Create this authentic parchment map and instead of giving someone a present, pop it inside the treasure chest and make them hunt for it!

From paper to parchment

Materials

White paper

Stock cubes

Small bowl

Bread   Paint

Paintbrush

Marker pen

Gold pen

Make sure the stock is nice and thick.

Don't be frightened to flick quite hard. The tears need to be noticeable.

1 Make a sheet of paper look really old by tearing along all of the edges, don't worry about being neat! Flick around the outside to make a few small tears.

2 Take a bowl and crumble a stock cube into it. Add enough water to make a thick mixture and paste it on to your paper with your fingers. It will look better if you rub it in roughly. Let it dry.

Make sure you don't put the paint on too thickly.

A gold pen looks very effective on the red.

3 To make a fancy stamp, take a piece of bread and cut it into a small square. Paint some red poster paint on to it and press it down, not too heavily, in the corner.

4 When the paint is dry, draw a symbol, or a letter if you are writing a message, on top of it. Draw a symbol that has something to do with the theme. In this case, a treasure chest.

'X' marks the spot

What a fantastic way to give someone a present! When they receive the map, they will have no idea what it is. Watch while the person hunts for their gift, but don't give away any clues!

Map it out

Make sure that you walk around the area where you hide the gift and draw the map as accurately as possible. To make it harder, make a bigger map with more landmarks.

Use brighter paints for a bolder map!

To make the rolled-up map effective, you will need to paste both sides with the stock mixture.

Draw on extra features such as this galleon.

Turn your house and garden into an island on the map to give it a 'treasure island' look!

Treasure hunt

When you present the map, roll it up and tie a ribbon around it, to make it look like an ancient parchment.

If the present is for a birthday you could make a message tag.

5 Now it is time to draw your map. Work out where you will hide your treasure chest and make a map of the area. Put in landmarks that are recognizable, such as trees, a house, or a shed.

6 When you have drawn your map in marker pen, decorate it lightly using poster paints. Make sure your 'x' is shown clearly in the right spot.

PEEP-PROOF BOX

Trouble with snoopers? What you need is a peep-proof box! Keep your secrets safe by giving curious hands an unpleasant surprise!

From box to shocks

Materials

Cardboard box, bin-liner, and tinsel

Sticky tape   Paint

Small boxes and tubes

Sticky tack   String

Scissors

Pencil

Paintbrush

Marker pen

Position a piece of sticky tack behind the hole so that the pencil will go through smoothly and safely.

If you make the hole bigger than your fist, anyone will be able to enter the box!

1 Take a cardboard box and securely tape up the bottom, leaving the top open. Place your fist on one side of the box and draw around it.

2 Cut the hole out – start by pushing a pencil through the cardboard to make a small hole. Make sure the hole is no bigger than your fist.

Attach the boxes securely with lots of sticky tape.

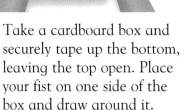

3 To make the secret compartments, take some small boxes and tubes and stick them to the inside of the box. Pop your top secret items inside them.

When the flap flips over, the dangly bits will hang just behind the hole.

4 Now you need some unpleasant dangly bits! Use sticky tape to attach string, tinsel, and shredded bin-liners to the inside of the flap above the hole.

Make sure the monster is unwelcome-looking to snoopers!

If you need to paint on top of the tape, mix poster paint with a little PVA glue.

5 Secure the lid of the box down with lots of sticky tape. With a marker pen, draw an outline of a monster face on the outside of the box using the hole as its mouth.

6 Paint your monster's face with lots of brightly-coloured poster paint. Greens and oranges are good monster colours! Paint the teeth white.

Monster protection

Now you have a peep-proof box that only your hand will fit in to! And if someone does try to snoop they will come across a very unpleasant surprise!

Try sticking on Ping-Pong balls for the bulging eyes!

Who would want to risk putting their hand into this monster mouth?

Jaws

This vicious-looking shark is guaranteed to protect your secret belongings, especially with its extremely unpleasant dangly curtain!

TIDY HIDEAWAY

Hmake this mailbox desktidy with a difference
– lots of extra hiding places for your trinkets!

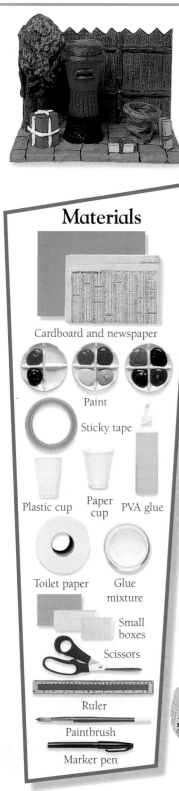

Materials

Cardboard and newspaper

Paint

Sticky tape

Plastic cup

Paper cup

PVA glue

Toilet paper

Glue mixture

Small boxes

Scissors

Ruler

Paintbrush

Marker pen

From board to hideaway

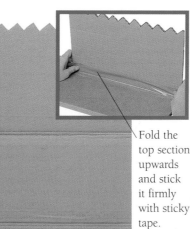

Fold the top section upwards and stick it firmly with sticky tape.

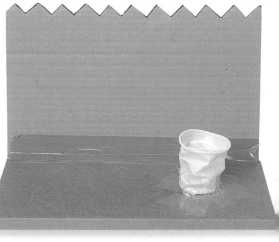

1 Take a long rectangle of cardboard and divide it equally into three with a ruler. Cut a zigzag along the top end. Fold the bottom section on top of the middle section and glue it down with PVA glue.

2 To make a postbag, take a plastic cup and press the top down with your hand, to make it look squashed. Attach it with sticky tape.

Cover the lid separately.

5 To make the parcels, gather together some small boxes, such as empty matchboxes or small sweet boxes. Use sticky tape to attach them to the base, but make sure you don't stick them closed!

6 Slop some PVA glue mixture on to the surface and lay strips of toilet paper all over the top. Make sure you can still open the boxes, however!

Attach the two cardboard pieces together with sticky tape and add some squashed newspaper to the larger circle. Put the lid to one side.

Twist the roll tightly between your fingers.

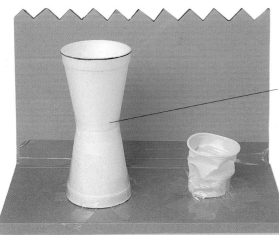

If you want a hollow postbox, before you stick them together carefully snip holes in the bases of the cups or get an adult to help you.

3 Take two paper cups and attach them, bottoms together. Stick them to the base with sticky tape. Make a lid by drawing around the top of a cup on to a piece of cardboard, cut it out. Cut out another circle half a cm smaller, see insert above.

4 Attach a tree to the base by rolling a tube of newspaper tightly and wrapping it with sticky tape. Squash a ball of newspaper in your hand for the top and attach it to the trunk.

Use black marker pen to draw guidelines for painting.

7 Dip some scrunched up pieces of toilet paper into the PVA glue mixture, squeeze out the excess, and add some pulped 3-D effects to the features such as the postbox, tree, fence, and parcels.

8 When the scene is completely dry it is time to paint it! Use poster or acrylic paint and make sure you use really bright colours. Paint the postbox bright red and the picket fence brown.

TIDY HIDEAWAY

What better way to hide something special than to conceal it amongst your pencils and paper-clips in this spectacular desk tidy!

Paint branches and leaves on your tree.

The lid should look as if it can't be removed when it is on the postbox – making it a fantastic place to hide your secrets.

The black marker pen gives the picket fence a great wood effect.

Safekeeping

When the paint is dry, highlight some areas with a black marker pen to finish it off. Pop your stationery into your desk tidy to disguise the fact that you have your secret trinkets hidden in the postbox or one of the parcels!

If you don't keep your secrets in the postbox, keep your pens in it!

Neat and tidy
Now you have a desk tidy with boxes that open, a postbox with a lid for your secret belongings, and a postbag to fill with paper-clips or split pins! Keep sneaky fingers away from your things for good!

The little parcels will hold your tiny trinkets.

Make sure you paint the colours of the rainbow in the right order!

The grey pavement makes the scene look really street-like.

Over the rainbow
The simple models look just as good as the complicated ones. Create this rainbow tidy, with a corner of a cardboard box, complete with a pot of gold and piles of nuggets next to it!

Use either gold paint or gold pen to paint the nuggets.

You could adapt your model so that you can fit an alarm clock into it.

Rescue mission
There are so many scenes you could try out. You could even make a bedside tidy, such as this fantastic fire engine rescuing the cat from the upper window! It has a house, made from an old cereal box, that holds your alarm clock in the window and a hosepipe swirl that will hold a mug of water! Lift up the top of the fire engine and there you have your secret drawer!

Make the ladder with a piece of cardboard and a fireman's standing box with a matchbox.

The hosepipe is made out of rolled up newspaper.

21

STONE WARNING

Do you ever want privacy in your bedroom to discuss secret plans? Here's a way to ensure that everyone enters with caution!

From card to carving

Squeeze the two sides together to cut the 'v' shape.

Do not force the crunching too much or the box will tear.

Materials

Cereal box, white paper, and newspaper

Sticky tape   Paint

Toilet paper   Glue mixture

Scissors

Pencil

Paintbrush

Marker pen

1 Take an empty cereal box and snip some 'v' shape slits along the edges with a pair of scissors. Don't snip too many slots down each edge.

2 Stand the box up and crush it down to buckle the sides. Stuff the box with crunched-up balls of newspaper. Tape the top down securely.

3 Decide at this stage what you want to carve into your stone slab. It's a good idea to practise first on a piece of paper. Choose your style of writing carefully, you could try pointy-shaped letters, and write 'Beware Do Not Enter'.

BEWARE DO NOT ENTER

4 Cover the box with PVA glue mixture and lay strips of toilet paper on the front. Lay six or seven layers down on the front only and make sure they remain wet and pulpy while you are covering it.

Caution!

Put your ancient stone warning slab outside your bedroom door to bar the way of anyone entering. An aggressive message is guaranteed to work as a very effective warning!

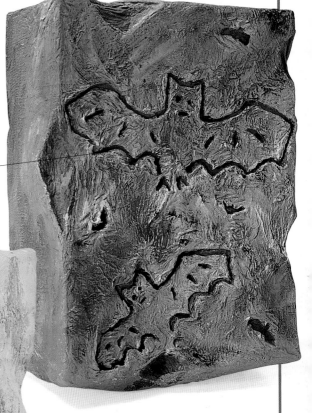

Highlighting the indentations with black pen really makes the message stand out.

For the best effect, use a darker version of the main colour in the carved areas.

Why not try carving pictures into your stone slabs?

Tomb raider

You would expect to find this sand coloured slab in an Egyptian tomb, complete with a mysterious message!

Bat mania

Try a dark sign like this vampire bat. It will ensure that unwelcome visitors will knock first!

5 While the pulp is still wet, carve the message into it, using a pencil. When you have finished, cover the rest of the box with PVA glue mixture and one layer of toilet paper. Leave it to dry.

6 When it is dry and rock hard you can make out the indentations of the carvings. Paint the surface using black and white acrylic or poster paints. Use darker paint in the carved grooves to highlight them.

WAX ILLUSION

Have you ever wanted to send a note to someone without anyone else reading it? Now you can, here is a fantastic way to send an invisible message!

From invisible to visible

Materials

A4 paper and newspaper

Wax crayons and coloured pencils   Paint

Old ballpoint pen

Paintbrush

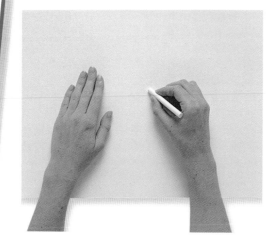

1 Take a piece of white paper and a white wax crayon. Write a message on the paper but don't worry if you can't see it – that's the whole point!

2 Use a coloured, watered-down poster paint to brush over the piece of paper. The message should appear loud and clear!

The thinner the paint, the more effective it will be.

Mystery message
Write a secret message and give it to a friend – but make sure they know how to read it! A wax message is a great way to ensure that a letter doesn't get into the wrong hands.

OUR SECRET CLUB MEETING WILL BE HELD IN THE GARDEN SHED AT 3.00 PM ON SATURDAY

INVISIBLE NOTE

What happens if someone finds out how to decipher the wax illusion? Don't worry – try this alternative invisible note writing instead!

From indent to illusion

The newspaper will ensure that you can press hard enough to make the imprint without damaging the table beneath!

1 Lay a piece of A4 paper on to an old newspaper. Take an old ballpoint pen that has run out of ink and press a message hard into the paper without tearing it.

2 Take a coloured pencil that is a different colour to the paper. Rub the pencil all the way across the message and the writing should appear clearly! Try to do the rubbing evenly.

Make sure the pencil and paper are contrasting colours.

Covering tracks

Now you can write your innermost secrets without anyone else being able to read them! Remember, however, to destroy the newspaper that you lean on – somebody might be able to pick up the message concealed in the newspaper!

The secret instructions are in the biscuit tin. Read and destroy!

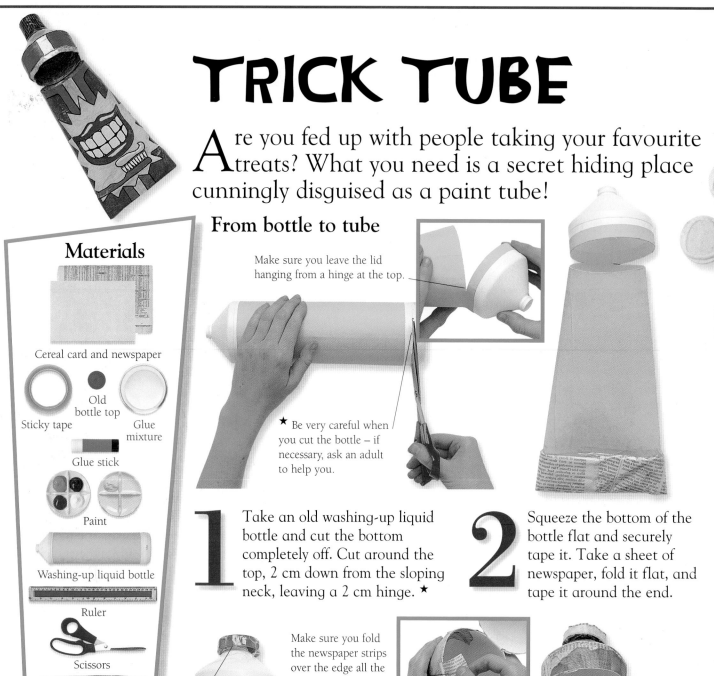

TRICK TUBE

Are you fed up with people taking your favourite treats? What you need is a secret hiding place cunningly disguised as a paint tube!

From bottle to tube

Make sure you leave the lid hanging from a hinge at the top.

★ Be very careful when you cut the bottle – if necessary, ask an adult to help you.

Materials

Cereal card and newspaper

Sticky tape

Old bottle top

Glue mixture

Glue stick

Paint

Washing-up liquid bottle

Ruler

Scissors

Paintbrush

1 Take an old washing-up liquid bottle and cut the bottom completely off. Cut around the top, 2 cm down from the sloping neck, leaving a 2 cm hinge. ★

2 Squeeze the bottom of the bottle flat and securely tape it. Take a sheet of newspaper, fold it flat, and tape it around the end.

You will have to use quite a lot of tape to secure it.

Make sure you fold the newspaper strips over the edge all the way around.

Build up about two or three layers of newspaper.

3 To make the top of the paint tube, take the lid off a plastic bottle and place it on top of the washing-up liquid bottle. Using sticky tape, secure it into place – try to be as neat as possible.

4 Take some PVA glue mixture and paste it on to the surface of the bottle. Tear strips of newspaper and put them all over the surface. It is very important to lay some longer strips over the edge of the opening.

It's amazing how
many sweets you
can fit inside
your tube!

Sun, sand, sea

This sun cream tube is a cunning disguise for a sweet hoard!

For a shiny effect, paint
the surface with PVA
glue – when it dries it
will be see-through.

Sweet tooth

A tube of toothpaste with a difference! There's no minty paste inside this one, just a great hiding place!

Safe and sound

Now you have the perfect place to hide your sweets. Leave it anywhere in your room and no-one will know that it opens and contains hidden delights!

Use silver pen or paint
for this metallic look.

Don't worry if your
collar is too long.

Half of the collar
should stick out
over the lip.

It is important to
remember to paint the
collar of the tube as well.

5 Cut a strip of card, about 3 cm wide, as a collar for the opening. Paste some glue stick around the top of the body of the tube and stick the collar on to it.

6 Paint the whole tube, one or two solid colours first and let it dry. You can then decorate with your own designs to make it look like a real paint tube.

ID BADGE

Are you a member of a secret club? If so, what you need is a secret club ID badge. Something that only you and other members will understand.

From board to badge

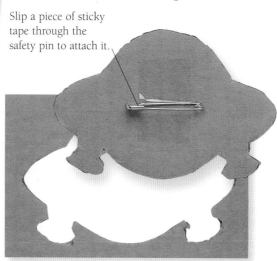

Slip a piece of sticky tape through the safety pin to attach it.

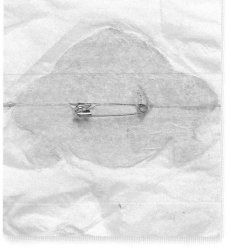

Materials

Cardboard

Sticky tape

Safety pin

Paint

Toilet paper

Glue mixture

Scissors

Paintbrush

Marker pen

1 Take a piece of cardboard and draw the badge shape on it with a marker pen. Attach a closed safety pin to the back with the pin fastening face up. Cut it out.

2 Paste the back with PVA glue mixture. Place one layer of toilet paper on either side of the pin. Let it dry and cut around the shape.

You will have to squeeze out the excess glue mixture when you dip it.

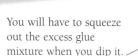

Make sure you use colours that stand out!

3 Take some clumps of toilet roll and dip them into PVA glue mixture. Stick the pulp on to the front for a 3D effect and smooth the surface down with your fingers.

4 The surface will dry hard and will be ready to decorate. Draw your design with a marker pen and then paint over it with poster or acrylic paints.

Secret UFO spotters club

It's fun to belong to a club that only
certain people know and understand,
and a badge can be a perfect way to
connect the members in the know!
Design some identical badges for
your secret club and wear
them with pride!

Black marker
pen gives a very
effective reflection
for the windows.

Don't make the badge
too big or it will be
too heavy to wear!

Use silver paint
to give the badge
a sparkling look.

Identity logo

Why not design your own logo for your club, or
if you don't have a secret club then start one! It's
best to keep the logo fairly simple but meaningful
to the members. It will be more eye-catching if
you use bold colours on an uncomplicated design.

This logo could be
something to do with
a secret eclipse club.

The leader of
the club could
have a slightly
different badge.

Rocket power

When you wear your badge only
your members will know what it
means. Keep the club a secret
and any inquisitive non-members
will be none the wiser!

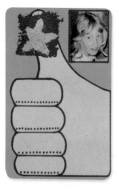

CLUB CARD

Now you have your secret club badges you need some form of official identification. Easy – simply make your own membership cards!

From card to club member

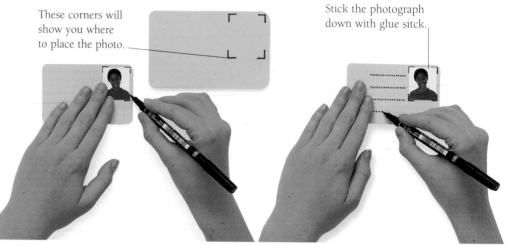

These corners will show you where to place the photo.

Stick the photograph down with glue sitck.

Materials

Thin card

Paint

Bread

Photo

Glue stick

Pencil

Ruler

Scissors

Marker pen

1 Cut a small rectangle out of thick paper or thin card, about the size of a credit card, and round off the corners. Take a small photograph of yourself and draw around the corners.

2 With a pencil, lightly draw four lines of equal distances across the card. Go over them with a marker pen, using dots rather than a thick line. Rub out the lines when the pen is dry.

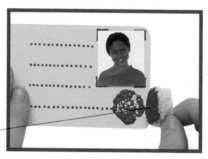

Dip a small piece of bread in paint to stamp the bottom right hand corner.

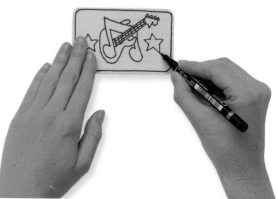

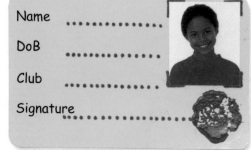

Name ....
DoB ....
Club ....
Signature ....

3 Write 'name', 'date of birth', 'club', and 'signature' down the left hand side of the card. Make a stamp in the bottom corner using a small piece of bread.

4 Decorate the back by drawing a design based on the theme of the secret club. When you have finished you can hand the cards out to the club members for them to fill in.

Club class

Now you have your own personal membership card complete with the details of your club. You shouldn't give away too many details, however, you want to keep it as secret as possible! Don't let a card fall into the wrong hands!

The back should give a small clue as to what the club is all about.

Name	Cynthia Crane
DoB	1st April 1989
Club	The wiggle club
Signature	*Cynthia Crane*

Call your secret club a name that doesn't tell people exactly what it is!

Covering up

You could always cover your official club card with sticky-backed plastic. This will help to preserve it and make it waterproof.

You can either use a passport photo or you can cut your head out of a larger picture.

Try using two colours for your stamp.

Use poster paints to add different colours to your cards.

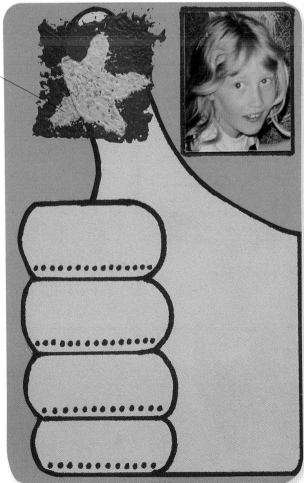

Key features

Membership cards come in all shapes and sizes. Why not try this key shape, the odder the shape the more it will mystify anyone who dares try and question the club without being invited to!

Thumbs up!

This handy image is perfect for an official card. Why not make up a password or even a special sign, such as this 'thumbs up' to alert other members to the fact that you belong to the same club.

PRIVATE EYE

Have you ever wanted to make sure that no-one recognizes you? Here's a great way to disguise yourself, your very own spy mask!

From box to espionage

Materials

Cardboard and paper

Sticky tape

Paint

Toilet paper

Glue mixture

Scissors

Ruler

Paintbrush

Marker pen

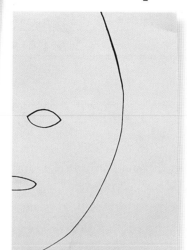

Finish the line off by drawing across the top.

1 Take an A3 piece of paper and fold it in half. Starting at the folded edge, draw half a face, making sure that it is the length of your face. Cut it out.

2 Turn a cardboard box upside-down and fold the open paper mask over a top corner. Draw around the mask shape, and carefully cut the shape out.

Copy this shape to use as the collar, which will bend around the mask.

Collar

Hat rim

Stick the hat rim around the mask above the eyes.

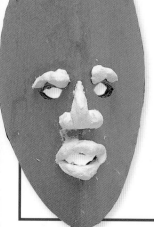

3 To make the 3-D features, take some toilet paper and dip it into PVA glue mixture. Squeeze out the excess glue and mould it into some eyebrows, a nose, and a mouth shape on your mask.

4 To make the hat rim, turn the mask upside-down and draw around the forehead angle on to a piece of cardboard. Draw a half circle around it, as above. For the collar, measure the widest point across the mask and draw the shape of a collar on cardboard, making sure that it is wider than the mask. Cut the shapes out. Attach them using sticky tape.

Before you paint the mask, you could always stick on a layer of tissue paper with glue mixture for a really smooth finish.

5 Once the surface is dry, you can paint the mask. For the face, try to copy the colour of your arm. Use a few colours but mix a little at a time and keep adding until you reach the perfect shade.

Fold down the top of the collar.

Your eyes will look really eerie through this masked face!

The beard and moustache are made with the 3-D pulp.

Use marker pen to highlight areas of the mask such as the eyes or the collar.

Undercover antics

Now you can transform yourself into a true detective with this fantastic, dodgy-looking disguise! Practise trailing a member of your family around your house, make sure they don't notice you are following them at any time!

Face of Zorro

There are lots of shady characters that you can make into a mask. This Zorro mask would be perfect to hide behind.

HEART THROB

Do you spend all day thinking about your pin-up? Do you want somewhere special to hide their photo? Well stop thinking and get making!

From paper to pin-up

Write an 'S' in the third square along.

Materials

Thin card

Paint

Glue stick

Photo

Ruler

Scissors

Pencil

Paintbrush

Silver and gold pens

Marker pen

1 In order to make an arrow for the heart throb, take a piece of thin card and draw around a ruler using a pencil or a marker pen.

2 Divide the outline into three equal parts and then divide the centre portion into three again. Mark an 'S' in the third small box.

Mark the points of the red box only and draw it on to the heart.

Make sure you paint the box to the left of the photograph red.

Glue the photograph on with glue stick.

3 Draw an arrowhead on one end of the arrow and a feathery tail on the other. Decorate the arrow making sure you put the photograph into the box marked 'S'. Paint the centre box red, as shown. Cut the shape out.

4 Place the arrow on a piece of paper and draw a heart shape around it, wider than the middle section. Draw around the arrow within the heart.

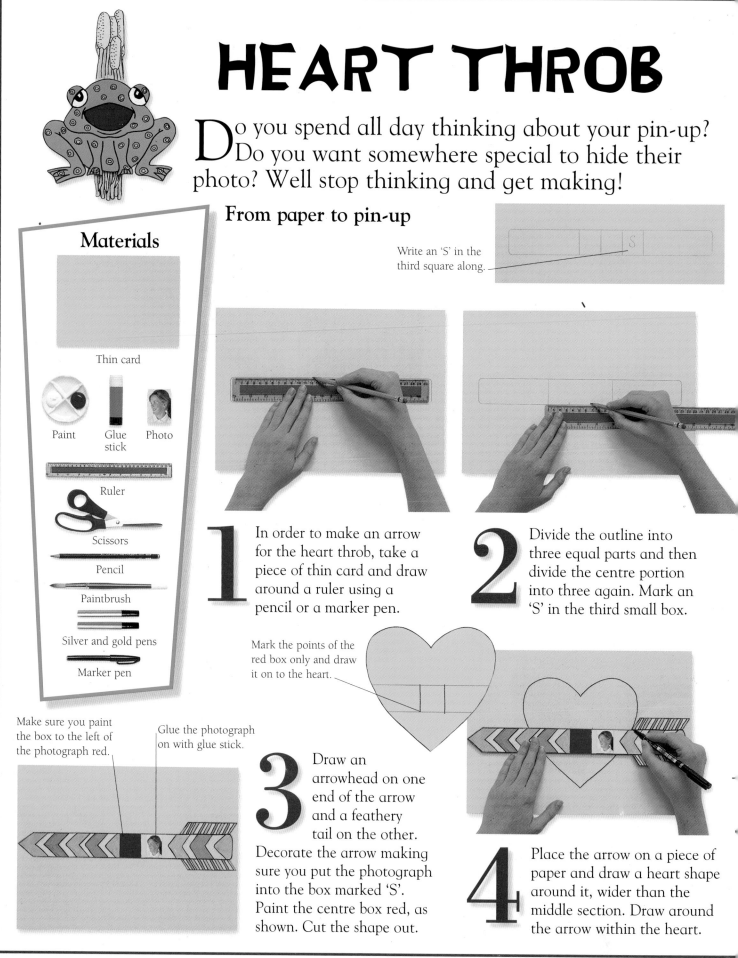

Heart-breaker

No-one will ever know that the heart throb contains your secret pin-up! Now all you have to do is pull the arrow whenever you want a peep!

Line the red box up with the heart and the photo is hidden.

The bullrushes behind the toad make a very good arrow substitute.

Toad in the hole

Alternatively you could write 'guess who' in the 'S' box and send it as a mystery valentine card to your secret pin-up!

Why don't you pop a fly in the mouth of the toad as well?

You will have to find a very big envelope to fit your heart throb!

Close to the heart

When the picture is hidden, the red box on the arrow will blend into the heart and hide the fact that there is anything beneath.

If the arrowhead doesn't quite fit, you could always snip the slots a little bigger.

Weave the arrow through the heart carefully.

Cut these lines to make the slots.

5 Cut the heart shape out. Carefully cut down the two lines of the box from top to bottom so that they make small slots. These slots are where the arrow will go through.

6 Paint the heart the same red as the box on the arrow and let it dry. Thread the arrow through the slots starting from beneath the heart threading upwards through the slot, then down through the next one.

SECRET CODES

Ｈow would you like to make a completely
decipher-proof code that only you and your
best friend will be able to read? Now you can!

From card to code

Make the marks at 12 degrees,
24, 36, 48, 60 and so on until
you reach the end.

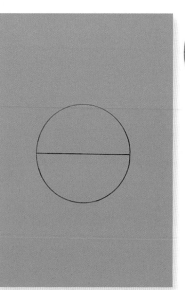

Make sure the
line goes straight
through the
centre.

Materials

Thin card

Paint

Sticky tack

Split pin

Compass

Protractor

Scissors

Ruler

Pencil

Paintbrush

Marker pen

1 Take a piece of thin card and
draw a circle on it with your
compass. Mark the centre,
and draw a line through the
middle. Cut the circle out.

2 Place a protractor on the
centre line and mark at 12
degree points around the
circle. Turn it upside down
and mark the rest of the circle.

The larger circle
should be about 2 cm
larger around the edge
than the small one.

3 When you have
marked the
circle all the
way around,
take a ruler
and draw a line from
the centre of the circle
to each of the marks.
When you have finished
make another larger disc
in exactly the same way.

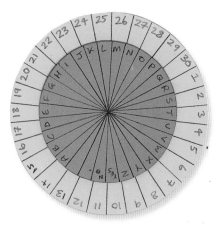

4 On the big wheel write the numbers 1-30
in each gap. In the small wheel write the
letters A-Z and in the four gaps write 'no',
'yes', a 'fullstop' and leave one blank.

Code wheel

Now that you have your decorated secret code wheel all you need to do is work out how to use it! Turn the page to find out how to send messages that not even the cleverest of code-breakers will be able to decipher!

You could use coloured pens or pencils as well as paint to decorate.

Love wheel

If you use the secret code to send a secret message to a loved one, why not design a heart wheel like this one? You could use a silver pen for the numbers to make it really special!

It is very important that the 12 degree gaps are measured accurately so that the wheels match up.

Use a sharp pencil to make a clear hole.

Use poster or acrylic paints for the decoration.

Split the pin at the back of the circles.

5 Punch a hole through the middle of both of the circles with a pencil. Place a ball of sticky tack behind the cards when you poke the pencil through. Join them together with a split pin.

6 Now you have your secret code maker, you need to decorate it! Create your own design and paint it. Go over the numbers and letters with a marker pen.

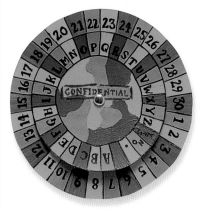

SECRET CODES

To make this brilliant code wheel work, your best friend will have to make one as well. You will need two exactly the same.

Code setting

When you have a code wheel each, you will be able to set the code with your friend. To translate your message, your friend will have to use the same code as when you wrote the note. On this wheel the code is set on **1** and **P**, so 1 equals the letter **P**. Now it is ready to use! Write a message using the numbers around the edge that apply to their corresponding letter. When you want to write a new word go to where the space is, here it is 15. You will now have a message written with just numbers!

Crack the cipher!

Your friend will be able to translate the message simply by using the same code setting on their wheel, which you have arranged beforehand. This message was set with the code wheel on the right. Practise a message using this wheel!

The letter 'J' will be written as '25'.

The '10' is a 'Y' on the code wheel.

5, 23, 20, 15, 1, 16, 4, 4, 8, 30, 3, 19, 15, 24, 4, 15, 26, 20, 10

THE PASSWORD IS KEY

! In on the secret
It is very important to tell your friend the code setting. Why not write the setting in the corner of the message?

5, 23, 20, 15, 1, 24, 22, 20, 30, 29, 15

23, 16, 4, 15, 27, 20, 21, 5, 15, 5, 23, 20

15, 18, 30, 30, 1, 14, 15

28, 20, 4, 4, 16, 22, 20, 15, 5, 30, 15, 18, 30, 28, 20

Brain teaser

To practise deciphering, try working out this long message using the settings on the heart wheel to the left. The answer is under 'Message 1' at the bottom of the page.

Hieroglyphic wheel

You can also make a wheel with pictures and letters, instead of numbers. Try making this ancient Egyptian hieroglyphic wheel! Write a picture message to someone and if anyone else finds it there is absolutely no hope of them cracking the code unless they have the wheel and the setting!

I LOVE YOU

You can choose any picture you want!

Picture codes

Here is an example of a simple picture message, use the egyptian wheel to crack it and check your answer below!

FORBIDDEN FILE

Do you have any private notes that you don't want anyone to see? If so, you need a secret file, or a secret compartment in a secret file!

From card to compartment

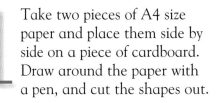

Use a long strip of sticky tape and curl it over the edge of the cardboard.

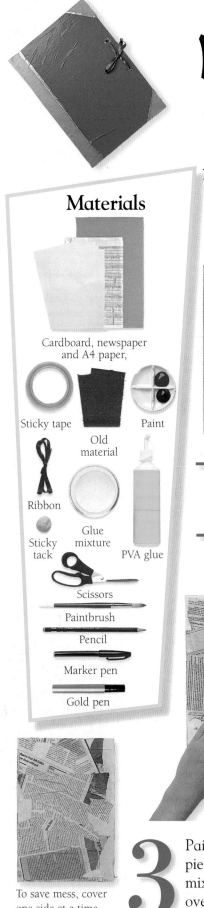

Materials

Cardboard, newspaper and A4 paper,

Sticky tape

Old material

Paint

Ribbon

Sticky tack

Glue mixture

PVA glue

Scissors

Paintbrush

Pencil

Marker pen

Gold pen

1 Take two pieces of A4 size paper and place them side by side on a piece of cardboard. Draw around the paper with a pen, and cut the shapes out.

2 Lay a piece of A4 paper on each piece of cardboard and tape them down. Only tape the top, bottom, and one side. Leave one side open.

Don't be too neat when you lay on the strips – the wrinklier the better!

When the PVA glue dries it will be hard and shiny.

To save mess, cover one side at a time and let it dry!

3 Paint both sides of the cardboard pieces, or file flaps, with PVA glue mixture. Stick strips of newspaper all over both sides. Be very careful not to paste over the pocket openings.

4 When the file flaps are dry, paint them with brown paint for a leather effect. When they are dry, cover them with PVA glue, which will dry see-through.

Make sure there is a gap of about 1 cm between the flaps, so that the file will close.

Cut triangular pieces of material out for the corners and stick them on with PVA glue.

The ribbon should be long enough to tie a secure bow.

Make sure you use a sharp pencil to pierce the holes, but be very careful.

5 Place the two flaps side by side with the open pockets facing each other and the cardboard sides facing up. Lay a piece of material, about 4 cm wide, down the centre. Stick it down with PVA glue.

6 Pierce two holes with a pencil, using sticky tack to push in to, along the edges where the file opens. They should be roughly 5 cm apart and about 2 cm in from the edge. Thread a piece of ribbon through the holes.

For your eyes only

To finish the edges off neatly, use a gold pen to draw lines around the material and the holes. Paint 'Top Secret' on the front with acrylic paint to deter anyone curious enough to look at the contents. But even if they do take a peep, they won't spot the top secret compartments with your top secrets inside!

Splat attack!
Try your own designs, this Art Attack splat file is a perfect place to keep all your Art Attacks – You can hide the ones you will give away as presents!

You could use a stencil to give it a stamped look.

Gold and silver pen give a really good sparkly look!

Peeping Tom
Private documents will be safe and sound! No prying eyes will ever think to look for secret sleeves inside a file!

41

DIARY DISGUISE

Do you write a diary that is strictly for your eyes only? Here's a solution – make a book tied with a chain and padlock!

From diary to disguise

Materials

Book

Toilet paper

Glue mixture

Paint

Pencil

Paintbrush

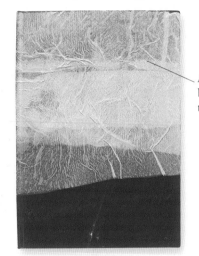

A hardback book works the best.

1 Take an exercise book and lay some strips of toilet paper all over the surface. Paste some PVA glue mixture on to the paper so that it sticks firmly.

2 When it is dry you can start your design. With a pencil, draw a chain across the book to make it look as if it is firmly locked shut.

! Squeezing tip
Squeeze the excess glue mixture out of the pulp before you use it.

Add pulp in the corners as well.

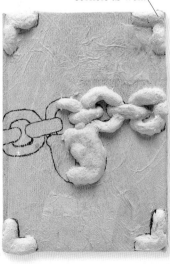

3 Take some more strips of toilet paper and dip them into the PVA glue mixture. Use this pulp to make the design 3-D, carefully moulding each link of the chain.

Make sure you mould a padlock on to your chain.

4 When the pulp is dry, it will be rock hard. Use poster or acrylic paints to decorate it. Paint the chain silver or grey.

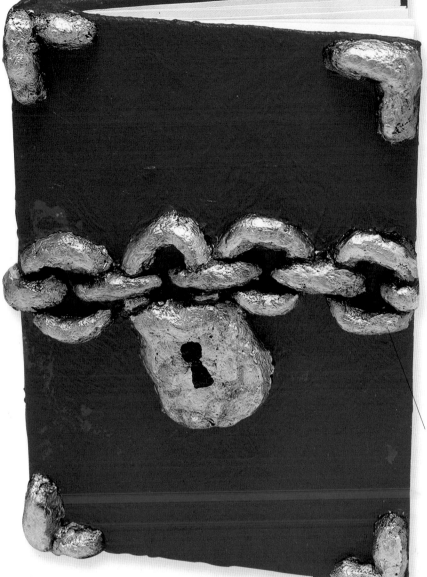

Under lock and key

This chain looks so convincing, it will deter anyone looking for your secrets! Make your own locked-up chain diary and keep your personal secrets well and truly under wraps!

Chain reaction

Decorate the back as well, so that the chain runs from the back of the book to the front.

Silver paint always looks effective as decoration.

Paint the book a good contrasting colour to the chain.

Jungle hoax

There are so many design ideas you can use to disguise your personal diary. Why not try this jungle theme and turn your diary into a bird book, complete with a patrol parrot protecting your private notes!

Use pulp for some of the leaves and then paint the rest.

Put your own telephone number on your book.

Phoney diary

What a brilliant disguise! Who would ever guess that a diary would be hidden inside a boring telephone book? Write some phone numbers on the first page to deter snoopers.

TOTEM POLE

Original totem poles were carved out of wood. Make your own with toilet rolls and use the hollow to hide your private notes inside!

Materials

Cereal card and cardboard

Paint

Sticky tape

3 toilet roll tubes

Toilet paper

PVA glue

Glue mixture

Scissors

Paintbrush

Marker pen

! **Totem design**

● Go to your local library and find some pictures of original North American totem poles to copy. They come in all sorts of wonderful designs.

From tube to totem

You will need the cardboard collars to stack your toilet rolls securely.

1 Make a cardboard collar by cutting a strip of cereal card, about 4 cm wide. Pop it into the top of a toilet roll tube and secure it down with PVA glue.

Keep the features simple but big for the best effect.

2 Draw a face, using a marker pen, on to your tube. The face can be as bizarre as you like. Original totem poles had some very strange features.

If you stick the nose down with sticky tape, you will need acrylic paints to paint on top of it.

3 To make the totem pole look carved, add some 3-D features to it. Cut out a diamond shape from a piece of cardboard and bend it in half for a nose. Stick it down with PVA glue or sticky tape.

After you dip the ball of toilet paper into the PVA glue mixture, squeeze it out a little so that it's not too soggy.

Attach the toilet paper balls to the tube securely.

4 Dip some scrunched-up pieces of toilet paper into PVA glue mixture and press them on to your tube. Mould them to the shapes you want as facial features, before they dry.

Don't worry if you put a lot of glue around the base, it will dry see-through.

Make the cardboard at least 10 cm by 10 cm to ensure that the totem stands up.

5 Leave the PVA glue pulp carvings to dry overnight. In the morning they should be rock solid – perfect for painting on to.

6 To make a base, you will need a thick piece of cardboard. Brush the bottom of your tube with PVA glue and stick it firmly to the middle of your base.

Make sure you exaggerate the features, such as the eyes and cheeks.

Remember to paint the collar as well so that the joins are less visible.

If you want to give your totem pole a shiny finish you can paint it with PVA glue.

The toilet roll should fit neatly around the collar of the one below.

7 Totem poles need some really bright colours! Use bright primary poster paints to make your totem pole really stand out. Exaggerate the features, such as the teeth and eyes using black marker pen.

 Pole tip
When you make your other two toilet rolls for stacking, add different facial features to each of them – make all of them unique.

8 When you have done two or three more toilet roll tube faces, slot them on top of each other using the cardboard collars to ensure that they hold together.

TOTEMS

Now all you have to do is pop a rolled-up private document inside the totem pole and you have a fantastic secret hiding place!

Make sure you attach the separate features, such as the wings, securely.

Family ties

Totem poles were thought to have been built by American Indians to represent their family spirits. Why don't you model one on your own family? You can use as many toilet rolls as you have members!

The eyes look better coloured white with black centres, they show up more.

Add details, such as these bird claws using black marker pen.

Elementary, my dear Watson

This Sherlock Holmes and Dr Watson totem pole will appeal to any budding sleuths! Set the most famous detective of all time the task of guarding your secret thoughts.

If you are making a personality, make sure you add something that will make them recognizable, such as this magnifying glass for Sherlock Holmes.

Totem deception

The hollow centre of the totem pole is perfect for slipping private letters into – and the taller the documents, the more sections you can add! You can even put them in any order you like!

It is important to have at least one tube with features that stick out, such as these ears.

Paint features on to your base such as the 'Hound of the Baskervilles' footprints.

Paint the base a bright colour that matches the colours on the totem pole.

Hat trick

It's a good idea to make a hat for your top figure so that no-one can tell that it's hollow. Then you really will be keeping your secrets under your hat!

Make the arms, with rackets or bats, separately and then tape them on afterwards.

Game, set, and match

There are lots of different themes you can use. This sporty pole is a winner! Whatever your sport or hobby is, try making a totem to match, putting the segments in any order you like!

Make sure your totem pole is tall enough to hide your documents.

47

JUMBLE JIGSAW

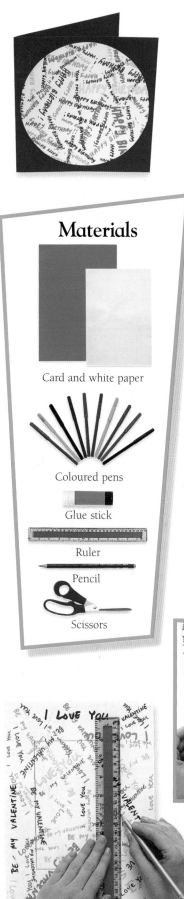

When it's Valentine's Day, are you a little bit shy when it comes to what to write in a card? Here's an answer – a jumble jigsaw!

From jumble to jigsaw

Materials

Card and white paper

Coloured pens

Glue stick

Ruler

Pencil

Scissors

Write the messages from lots of different angles.

1 Take a sheet of A4 paper and gather together as many coloured pens, pencils, and crayons as you can. Write your message across the paper.

2 Turn the paper and write the message all over in different directions. The more you write, the more difficult it will be to read.

You can write as many different messages as you like on the paper.

3 Using a ruler, draw a rectangle in the middle of your picture that will go on to your card. Cut it out, but don't throw away the rest of the message.

Stick the sheet any way up you like.

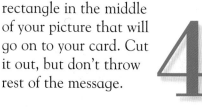

4 Fold a piece of thin card in half, making sure it is bigger than the rectangle you have cut out. Glue the message on to it.

The pieces can be any shape you want – the more complex the better!

Make sure you put all the pieces into the card. You don't want any gaps in the jigsaw!

5 Take the piece of paper that you didn't use and cut it into lots of pieces. You don't have to be particularly neat. This will make up the special jigsaw message!

6 Slip the pieces of paper into the centre of the card loosely, and send it to your valentine. When they receive it they will be able to piece it together to read the whole message.

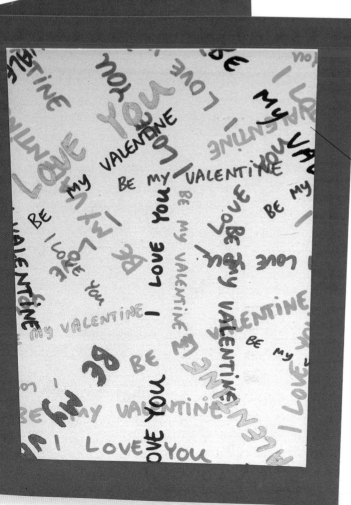

Use as many different coloured pens and pencils as you can to make it really bright.

Piece offering

What a surprise your valentine will get when the card opens and all the pieces fall out! And let's face it, if they go to those lengths to read your card, they must really fancy you!

You can cut out your message into any shape you want – why not try a star or a heart?

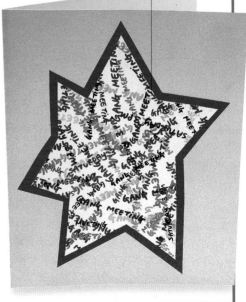

Cryptic message

Why don't you send your secret club members a jumble message and write the meeting place somewhere in the message for them to find?

DREAM ISLAND

Have you ever dreamed of owning a Caribbean island? A paradise in the sun? Now you can have your own custom-made secret hide-away!

From pulp to paradise

Materials

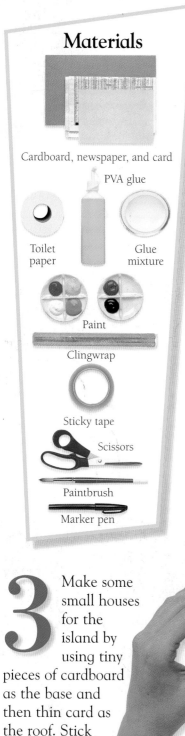

Cardboard, newspaper, and card

PVA glue

Toilet paper

Glue mixture

Paint

Clingwrap

Sticky tape

Scissors

Paintbrush

Marker pen

1 Take a piece of cardboard, draw a rough design of an island on to it with a marker pen, and stick scrunched up balls of newspaper on the top.

2 Paste some PVA glue mixture on to the surface of the newspaper and stick strips of toilet roll all over it. Smooth it down with a paintbrush.

Stick the houses on to the island with PVA glue.

3 Make some small houses for the island by using tiny pieces of cardboard as the base and then thin card as the roof. Stick them together.

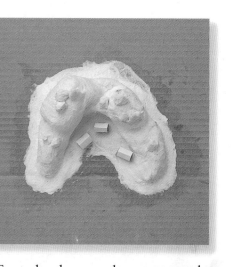

4 To make the tree shapes, scrunch up some tiny balls of toilet paper and glue them on the top. Brush glue mixture all over them and leave them to dry overnight.

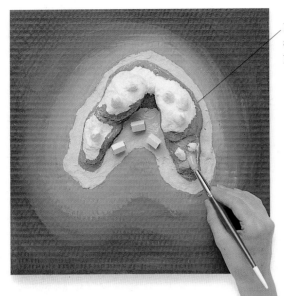

Make sure you paint all the little gaps in your island.

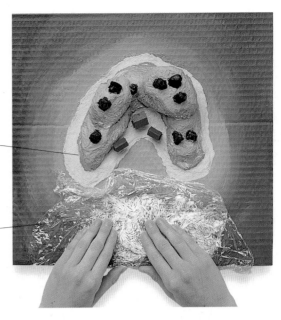

The cliffs should be lots of shades of grey.

When the glue mixture dries, the clingwrap will be see-through and will shimmer.

5 When the island is completely solid, it is time to paint it using poster or acrylic paint. Paint the sea using different shades of blues. Let it dry.

6 Take a sheet of clingwrap and tear it into small pieces. Brush some glue mixture on to the sea, stick on the clingwrap and wrinkle it up with your fingers to make waves.

Paradise found
With the sandy yellow beach and sparkling blue sea, your island really is a fantasy place. Create your own personal paradise.

Paint the sand a luscious beach yellow – perfect for paradise!

Make the steps out of little pieces of cardboard.

Pirate attack
Try creating a nightmare island, complete with skull-shaped cliffs. A place for pirates to plan attacks and hide their booty!

Mould the newspaper to make cave-like holes on your island.

Use little pieces of cardboard to make a pirate galleon.

Wrinkle up the clingwrap tightly to make crashing waves.

Ship ahoy!
Why not make some ships to float around your island? You could build a bright red and white lighthouse to guide ships at night.

SECURITY SPIDERS

Most people hate hairy, scary spiders especially on slippery webs! They are, therefore, the perfect security guards for your secret drawers.

From scrap to spiders

Make sure that all the legs are in the right position before you let them dry.

Materials

White, red, and black paper

PVA glue

Paintbrush

Marker pen

1 Take a piece of thin, black paper and screw it into a ball the size of your fist. Take eight more pieces and twist them into sausage shapes.

2 Dip each sausage leg into some PVA glue and stick it firmly into the body. Make sure the leg is embedded into the ball. Let the PVA glue dry.

Press the eyes firmly on to the body and let the glue dry.

Draw little black pupils on the white eyes with a marker pen.

3 Screw up two small balls of white paper for the eyes and glue them on to the body with PVA glue. Cut an oval shape from a piece of red paper and stick it on as a tongue.

4 Now for the messy bit! Cover the whole of your spider with PVA glue. Don't worry if it looks white, it will be hard, shiny, and see-through when it is dry.

Security alert

Yuk! Now your scary spiders are ready to hang on guard, but what you really need is a web. Turn over to the next page and find out how to make a shiny, white web for your ferocious spiders to sit on.

Make some bushy eyebrows out of small pieces of black paper.

Big, white teeth automatically make a spider look aggressive!

The PVA glue coating makes the spider's body firmer.

Arachnophobia

Ideally you need someone in your family to be an arachnophobe – terrified of spiders. They will definitely be too frightened to pry in your private drawers!

Mellow yellow

This little spider's droopy eyes make it look half asleep – but you won't catch him off guard!

Give the spider exaggerated facial features by using marker pens and poster paints.

! **Paint tip**
If you want to paint the spider crazy colours, make sure you do it before you add the PVA glue. The hard coating needs to be the last layer.

Remember that spiders have eight legs!

The spiders look great as just decoration if you don't want them to guard your property.

Striped terror

Why not try making a really bright spider like this pink and black striped one? It looks really effective when it sits on its web.

WEB SITE

To make sure your spiders do the job efficiently, they will need something nasty to sit on. Take your PVA glue and make a wibbly-wobbly web!

From PVA to protection

Materials

Cardboard and white paper

Bin-liner

Sticky tape

PVA glue

Thick marker pen

1 Draw a spider's web on a piece of paper. Start with a large cross in the centre of the paper and work around it.

2 Take a piece of cardboard, place the drawing of the web on top of it, and then stick a large sheet of bin-liner on the top.

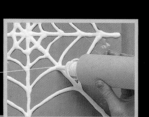

Keep the nozzle close to the surface for a thick line.

If you find a gap, go over it again with the glue.

3 Take a PVA glue bottle with a nozzle top and carefully draw over the web making sure that there are no gaps in the web. Leave it to dry overnight.

4 When the web is dry it will be solid. Carefully peel it off the plastic making sure you don't tear it.

The spiders will hang on to the webs if you curl the legs through them.

Web watch
Now that your spiders have webs, they are ready to get to work. Lay the webs over your drawers or boxes and strategically place the spiders on top. Who would want to break through this maze of spiders?

To make a green web, mix some green paint into the PVA glue pot.

This sparkly, silver one is made by pouring glitter on top of the drying web.

After a few days the white webs will go completely see-through.

Boxed in
It is unlikely that anyone will want to sneak past your vicious-looking spiders on their slippery, slimy webs!

SUPERSPY

Have you ever wanted to be a spy? Well now you can. Make this spy disguise complete with equipment and hidden pockets!

From box to disguise

Make two holes, as shown, by holding a piece of sticky tack behind the panel and sticking a pencil through.

Measure your side panels, which need to be half the size of the centre panel, and cut off the excess cardboard.

Materials

Cardboard box and cereal card

Paint

Sticky tack

Sticky tape

Scissors

Paintbrush

Pencil

Marker pen

Look at your school jacket for design ideas.

1 Take a cardboard box and cut away the top, bottom, and one large side. Measure halfway across the centre panel. Use this measurement for the side panels.

2 Fold the side panels in and cut away the whole of the top corners. Cut a 'v' shape down the edges of the side panels only.

The Hawaiian look makes a good casual disguise underneath the jacket.

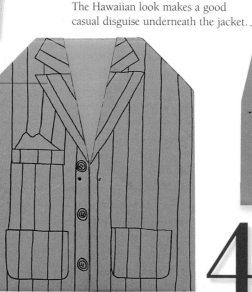

3 Make a rough design of a school jacket on the front panels, with black marker pen. Make sure you put on pockets, a collar, and buttons!

4 Open up the panels and draw the design of a shirt on the middle panel only. Draw a medallion around the neck where a spy might keep a small hidden camera!

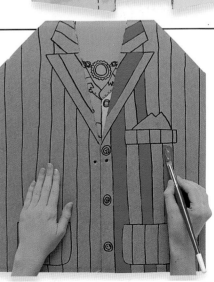

On a mission
All you need is a little spy imagination and you have your very own spy outfit! Try inventing equipment that you think spies might find useful on their missions.

Maps and secret messages are perfect for putting into the pockets!

Undercover agent
The beauty of the superspy is that it's lifesize so you can use it as a cunning fancy dress, but you could also loop a ribbon through the holes and use it as a secret file!

Design a really loud tie to go with your outfit!

Spy mac
There are many different disguises you can try. Create your own designs, such as this suspicious-looking macintosh!

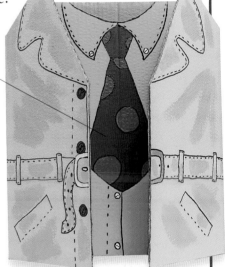

Draw real spy equipment in the pockets, such as a camera or binoculars!

Stick the sides and the bottom of the pockets down with sticky tape.

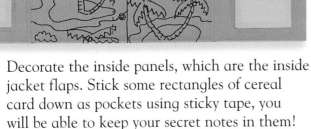

5 Decorate the inside panels, which are the inside jacket flaps. Stick some rectangles of cereal card down as pockets using sticky tape, you will be able to keep your secret notes in them!

6 Paint the outside of the jacket first using poster or acrylic paint. When it is dry, paint the inside as well. Use lots of bright colours as decoration.

BAT AMBUSH

Intruders in your room are a big worry. If you can't keep unwanted visitors out, then make their visit very unpleasant with these slimy bats!

From board to bat

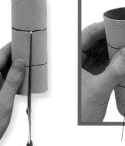

The slots should be exactly opposite each other.

Use sticky tape to tape up the sides of the 'v' shape so that the end lies flat.

Materials

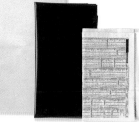

Cereal card, black bin-liner, and newspaper

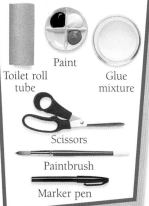

Sticky tape

Toilet paper

Paint

Toilet roll tube

Glue mixture

Scissors

Paintbrush

Marker pen

1 With a marker pen, divide a toilet roll tube into three equal parts. Cut a slit up either side of the tube, two thirds of the way up.

2 Squash the unsplit end together, with the splits on either side, and cut a 'v' shape within the first marked section. Tape the 'v' shape end.

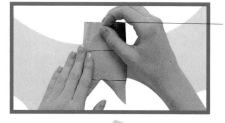

The tape should close up the slots above the wings to keep them in place.

! **Wing tips**
When you draw the wings make sure they are exactly the same size so that the bat is balanced.

6 Screw up a ball of newspaper and tape it into the end as a head. Dip some balls of toilet paper in glue mixture and stick them on top of the head as eyes. Cut some ear and foot shapes out of cereal card.

5 Take the body and slot the wings between the body slits as shown. Make sure the centre of the wings is in the centre of the body to ensure that the bat doesn't hang lopsided! Tape them into place.

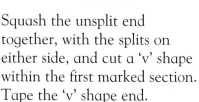

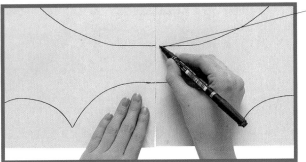

When you have drawn the wings, take off the bat body and join up the lines to the edge of the paper.

Tape both sides of the card a few times.

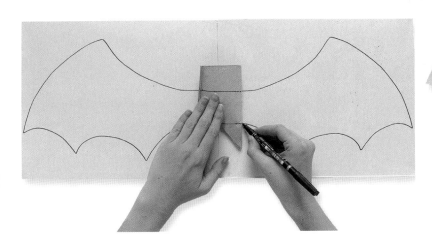

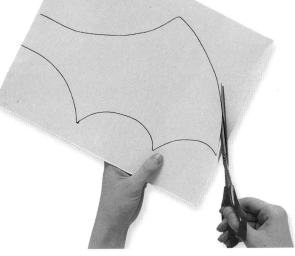

3 Place two pieces of cereal card next to each other and put the bat's body on to the centre, with the 'v' shape facing downwards. Mark the middle section of the tube on the card and, using the marks, draw the bat's wings.

4 Cut the wings out carefully from each card and lay them side by side. Tape them together, making sure you tape the front and the back of them to make them more secure.

Paint the underside of the wings as well.

8 When the paint is dry, draw around the wings on to a bin-liner and cut the shapes out. Stick the bin-liner to the top of the wings with PVA glue for a shiny, slimy effect.

Don't worry if the bin-liner is slightly wrinkled in places.

7 When the eyes are dry and you have finished your extra trimmings, paint the bat using black poster or acrylic paint. Make sure, however, you leave the eyes white.

BAT AMBUSH

These slimy bats can be customized to any design you want, ready to fly in the face of anyone who dares enter your room!

To give a sparkly wing effect, paste some PVA glue on to the wing and sprinkle some glitter on it.

Give the bats a vampire mouth complete with fangs!

Vicious vampire

When you have an army of bats, attach some string to their backs with sticky tape. Ask someone to help you hang them from the ceiling so that when a prowler opens the door and tiptoes into your room they will get a face full of flying bats!

Paint the inside of the big bat ears a different colour.

Bat attack

The bats look very alarming when they are hanging with just a tiny amount of light in the room. In moonlight they look really eerie. Why not try making the eyes with red reflective paper to make them shine in the dim light?

Remember to paint the underneath of the bat as well.

The lines on the wings make them look like the veins on real bat's wings.

! **Window watch**
The bats also look fantastic in front of a window. When the sun sets and it begins to go dark outside, they have a spooky silhouette!

Paint the wings with a bright colour if you want them to show up more.

To make a really effective flying army, you will need at least three bats – the more the better!

Imagine the flappy feel of a bat wing in your face as you open a door!

Dangerous danglies
Don't make the mistake of telling too many people about the trap, you want to make sure they never know what could be lurking behind closed doors!

Going batty
Remember bats sleep upside down, so make some sleepy ones and hang them by their feet from your ceiling.

The bigger and bulgier the eyes, the more they will look as if they are staring right at the intruder!

NEIL'S TIPS

With my book of secret Art Attacks, you are now fully equipped to handle all sorts of snoopers and pryers! But just before I go, here are a few more simple detective tips for you to try out. Be careful, however, to keep them under your hat!

Hair trick

One of the oldest tricks in the book is done with nothing more than a hair from your head! Pull out a hair, 'ouch', lick it, 'yuk', and carefully place it across the doors of a cupboard. If it has gone when you return, then you know someone has been snooping!

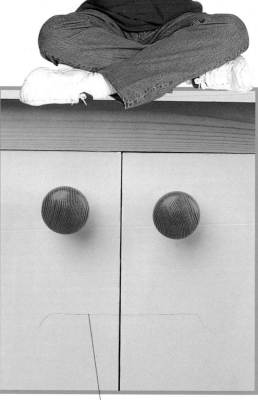

Make sure you stick the hair on either side of the doors.

Invisible ink

A brilliant way to do some invisible writing is with lemon juice. It is a very simple method, all you need is a paintbrush and a lemon! Send your message to a friend, but remember to tell them how to read it!

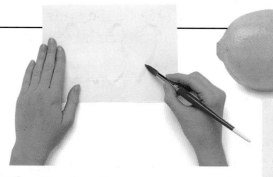

1 Simply write your message with lemon juice and let it dry. Send it to a friend and to read the message they will have to find an adult to help them iron it!

When you iron the message, the lemon juice will appear as if by magic!

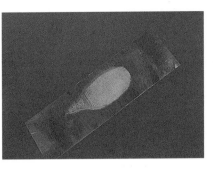

Sticky fingers

A clever way to find out if someone has been tampering with your belongings is the fingerprint test. Lightly shake some talcum powder on to a surface and you will see the prints. Put a piece of sticky tape over the top and then stick it on to dark paper – hey presto, a fingerprint!

Put the names of the members of your family above their prints.

Jackie's prints

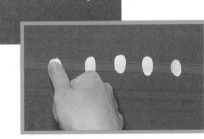

Taking prints

Take your family's prints, as well as your own, by making them dip their fingers into paint and printing them on paper. Compare the prints to the one you took and you have your culprit!

Eye spy

A brilliant and easy way to spy on someone is the simple newspaper trick. Just cut two holes in a newspaper, sit somewhere pretending to read it, while secretly watching what is going on around you!

INDEX